Government response to the Foot and Mouth Dise

GW00372492

Contents

Foreword by the Secretary of State for Environment, Food and Rural Affairs

Following the outbreak of Foot and Mouth Disease in 2007, the Prime Minister and I asked Sir Iain Anderson to conduct a review to see if the lessons of the 2001 outbreak had been learned and to recommend what further steps might be taken. As we saw in 2007, even when confined to a small number of infected premises in the same area, the impact of an outbreak can be considerable on the livestock sector, food businesses and the wider community.

I am grateful to Sir Iain for his review and for his recognition of how Government and the livestock industry tackled the outbreak in partnership. However, even though most things were handled well, I acknowledge that there are always lessons to learn and ways we can do better.

Since 2007, we have dealt with other exotic diseases, applying what we have learned, and as a result we are now better prepared. I am committed to continuing to work with the industry to ensure that this remains the case.

Introduction and background

1. Sir Iain Anderson's Review[1] commends the Government's overall handling of the 2007 Foot and Mouth Disease (FMD) outbreak, but there are lessons to be learned. Even when things have gone relatively well, Government needs to continue to develop its understanding of the risks, continue to improve preparedness for outbreaks, and work with industry to ensure that the risks of outbreaks are managed. Although the outbreak was small (confined to eight infected premises in Surrey and Berkshire), the impacts were felt across Great Britain.

2. The Prime Minister and Secretary of State invited Sir Iain to lead an independent review of the Government's response to the 2007 outbreak (Sir Iain chaired the inquiry into the 2001 outbreak[2]). Sir Iain was asked to establish whether relevant points from the Lessons to be Learned Report on the 2001 outbreak were implemented and to establish whether new lessons might be drawn from the handling of the 2007 outbreak.

3. This response describes how Government has learnt from its experiences in 2007 and is implementing the recommendations set out in Sir Iain's report. The Review made 26 recommendations grouped under eight of the nine lessons Sir Iain identified following the 2001 outbreak:-

    *   Maintain vigilance
    *   Be prepared
    *   React with speed and certainty
    *   Explain policies, plans and practices
    *   Respect local knowledge
    *   Risk assessment and cost benefit analysis
    *   Data and information management systems
    *   Base decisions on best available science

4. The response contains a range of actions, commitments and decisions. Some of the recommendations are multi-faceted and could not be implemented in full within the timescale of this response; in such cases the work in progress and directions for future work is reported. The response also comments on Sir Iain's two personal recommendations regarding the repositioning of the Institute for Animal Health and the creation of an Independent Advisory Committee on Animal and Emerging Infectious Diseases.

---

1   http://archive.cabinetoffice.gov.uk/fmdreview/
2   http://archive.cabinetoffice.gov.uk/fmd/

5. The Government will be consulting shortly on proposals to establish a new body, headed by an independent Chair and Board, operating at arm's length from Ministers that would assume all of Defra's existing roles and responsibilities in relation to animal health (animal welfare will remain a responsibility of Defra's and the Secretary of State). The consultation, which is in line with Sir Iain's previous Inquiry into the 2001 outbreak, will canvass views on proposals to require livestock keepers to contribute directly to the unbudgeted costs currently falling to Defra for dealing with outbreaks of exotic diseases, as well as providing matching funding for Defra's budgeted preparedness and surveillance work.

Lessons learned: Maintaining vigilance and being prepared

Progress on lessons learned

The Government welcomes the recognition that as a result of its action since 2001 the nation is now far more vigilant and aware of the threat posed by FMD. Better controls are in place to reduce the risk of exotic animal diseases entering the country through imports and contingency planning has undergone a step change in quality since 2001.

The experience of handling exotic disease incidents covering FMD, bluetongue and Avian Influenza in the past two years means Government is far better prepared than ever before. However, the Government is not complacent: Defra, the Animal Health Agency and others continue to learn and improve.

As a result of the FMD outbreak in 2007 Government is strengthening its approach to assessing disease risks and vulnerabilities and this is covered in more detail in the Chapter on Risk Assessment, Cost Benefit Analysis and Data. The UK Border Agency is a key and valued partner to help deter and detect illegal imports of animals and products which might harbour disease. Government will be vigilant about risk pathways within the UK. In response to the outbreak, the Government acted with speed to implement the recommendations made by the Callaghan Review to improve the regulatory framework for the handling of animal pathogens. Since April 2008, the Health and Safety Executive have been responsible for the inspection and enforcement of standards at Pirbright and other laboratories. Whilst some research with live viral animal pathogens has continued in certain buildings at IAH Pirbright, permission to work with these pathogens across the rest of the site will not be given until those containment facilities and standard operating procedures have been inspected by HSE and incorporated into a licence issued by Defra under the Specified Animal Pathogens Order 2008.

The Government's Responsibility and Cost Sharing agenda is building an effective partnership. Those with a common interest in managing exotic animal disease risks and limiting the impact of outbreaks for businesses and society generally are working together to apply their knowledge, skills and resources to deliver a mutually beneficial outcome. This vision of an effective partnership is illustrated very well by the work to limit the impact of bluetongue (BTV8). Government shares information about changes in risk. Solutions are developed with animal keepers, others along the food chain and the disease response operational partners. This enables all involved to develop and keep under review compatible contingency plans.

Review conclusions and recommendations

6. The Foot and Mouth Disease 2007 Review (the Review) concluded that Defra had taken many actions since the 2001 FMD outbreak to improve the vigilance it maintains in monitoring disease overseas and at the GB borders. The Review also reflected the success Defra and Animal Health have had in building emergency preparedness,

and mentioned that '*virtually all submissions received supported this view*'. However the Review makes a number of recommendations under the theme of maintaining vigilance and being prepared.

7. The Review recommends that Defra should continue to work with the UK Border Authority to maintain and strengthen vigilance, as well as consider the case for a standing zone around Pirbright with higher levels of surveillance and greater awareness-raising of the potential risk. The Review also calls for Defra to carry out more tests on the emergency response chain, as well as investigating/overhauling the ways in which Animal Health staff are trained in key skills, and how Regional Operations Directors and Divisional Operations Managers are utilised. In conjunction with this recommendation, Defra's existing contingency plans and emergency staffing models should be checked for their scalability. The Review recommended that more should be done to prepare generic licences for use in a future disease outbreak and that Defra should seek to increase the level of decision making it is possible to delegate to those on the ground, at the Local Disease Control Centre (LDCC), during an outbreak.

Vigilance

8. Defra's Framework Response Plan (FRP)[3] is the document that outlines the roles, responsibilities and procedures that are put in place to manage an exotic disease outbreak from the moment there is a suspected case of disease, to when Great Britain can be declared disease free. It is based upon strategic, tactical, and operational command and control principles and is aligned with established civil emergency response structures at local and regional level. The FRP is regularly revised and is subject to a public consultation prior to being laid before Parliament every year. There are similar plans for Scotland and Wales, and a shared recognition among the Great Britain authorities of the importance of close coordination.

9. The Plan does not detail the policies or disease control strategies that are implemented during an outbreak or the measures taken to prevent disease incursion into the country as these are set out separately on the Defra website. These include:

   • Intensified surveillance of animal disease
   • The management of legal intra-European Community and third country trade in animals or animal products
   • Measures to prevent the illegal import of animals and animal products
   • Improved biosecurity in farms and markets
   • General education and awareness in the farming and rural community of measures that can be taken to improve farm health and reduce risk of disease.

10. Close coordination between Defra, Animal Health, Devolved Administrations, Local Authorities, and other operational partners and stakeholders is required in the handling of an exotic disease outbreak. This is especially true in the case of FMD where the movement restrictions which were tightened in response to the 2001 lessons learned affect all of Great Britain, no matter how small the outbreak.

---

3   http://www.defra.gov.uk/animalh/diseases/control/contingency/exotic.htm

11. Preventing a disease outbreak is obviously preferable to controlling one. Defra has made improvements in the areas of vigilance, preparation and reaction since both the 2001 and 2007 outbreaks. These three areas are mutually dependant on each other; vigilance facilitates preparation, and preparation supports speed and certainty in response.

12. The Review recognised that Defra has been working with other government agencies and stakeholders to instil best practice import regimes since the 2001 outbreak. Defra continues to work closely with the UK Border Agency (UKBA) in the same manner as it had done with Her Majesty's Revenue and Customs (HMRC). One of the UKBA's key objectives is to reduce the risk of illicit import and export material that might harm the UK's physical and social wellbeing. Defra will support the UKBA by continuing to work on managing risk, as this will help to inform the UKBA on where they should focus their enforcement efforts. Defra, Animal Health, HMRC, and the UKBA will maintain ongoing public awareness campaigns in the UK and abroad as part of a joint publicity strategy. Defra will review and refresh these campaigns periodically to make sure they are up to date and reaching the intended audiences. The campaigns aim to raise awareness of the dangers of importing livestock and products of animal origin from countries where FMD is endemic. Novel approaches will be sought to make best use of the available resources.

13. Critical to strengthening vigilance, Defra will continue to work with the EU and at an international level to ensure compliance with EU and GB rules for commercial importation, as well as influencing other EU member states and third countries on minimising risk of introducing disease into the UK.

14. Livestock and poultry keepers, private vets, those involved along the food chain, as well as Government and its operational partners, all have a vested interest in preventing exotic disease outbreaks and limiting the spread of disease. Each has a role and responsibilities for which they are uniquely placed to deliver. Only through working together in partnership can high levels of vigilance and preparedness be achieved. The Core Group approach (see page 18) is more important than ever before as all stakeholders adapt to changes in climate which will increase the threat of exotic diseases spread by vectors which one cannot prevent coming into the country. Every stakeholder involved in the livestock industry needs to better understand the threats of exotic diseases and be able to spot them if they are to be identified and reported early. Guidelines on spotting clinical signs of disease and on the requirement to report a suspicious case are available on Defra's website. Industry bodies have invested wholehearted effort in supporting and promoting Defra's Give Disease the Boot campaign[4] which provides information on a range of diseases and advice on how best to protect the health of animals and the health of the farming industry. While industry have been taking a lead on campaigns such as the best practice guidance on free range turkey farming and the Joint campaign Against Bluetongue (JAB), Defra is committed to playing its part to build and strengthen the partnership by improving its understanding of the livestock and poultry sectors and associated industries.

---

4   http://www.defra.gov.uk/animalh/diseases/default.htm

15. A crucial part of preparing for a disease outbreak is training and awareness, combined with robust testing of the contingency plans through national and local exercises so that roles and responsibilities are well understood. Animal Health ensures that all elements of the emergency response chain are tested as part of their established exercise programme. The programme focuses on the key elements of the response and includes contingency contractors, stakeholders and operational partners. Key operational partners, such as local authorities, are also routinely involved. The entire emergency response chain is often not tested simultaneously, but rather certain sections of the response are selected to ensure that sufficient attention is paid to each element of the response and their connections to other elements and that learning is maximised. By the end of the 2008/9 financial year, Animal Health will have held 12 local or regional exercises involving every one of the Animal Health Divisional Offices.

16. The Defra Contingency Plan is reviewed annually and following a public consultation is laid before Parliament. As part of the latest review Animal Health is undertaking a critical review of the Government's outbreak response model in consultation with Defra and the Devolved Administrations. This review includes an assessment of the key skills and competencies required in Disease Control Centres, together with the development of an Animal Health skills register. Part of this review also included a reassessment of the roles Regional Operations Directors (RODs) and LDCC managers (formally known as Divisional Operations Managers) play in Local Disease Control Centres. The review has resulted in the creation of a new role of Regional Policy Advisor to support the ROD and to improve the communication of policy objectives between the LDCC and the NDCC. The latest version of Defra's Framework Response Plan reflects the new role. The review has also looked at information flows between the National Disease Control Centre (NDCC) and Local Disease Control Centres (LDCC) during outbreaks and incidents.

17. The 2007 FMD outbreak was confined to a relatively small area of Surrey and Berkshire, and as such only one LDCC was established. The Review raised the concern that had the outbreak been larger, requiring multiple LDCCs, perhaps Government would not have handled the outbreak so well. As the Review recognised, much has been done since 2001 to manage the risk of a large scale outbreak or multiple outbreaks. Notably the immediate imposition of a national movement ban until there is greater certainty about whether disease is present elsewhere. Resilience and scalability to handle a variety of exotic disease outbreaks were tested in 2007 when three different disease outbreaks were being handled simultaneously. In addition to FMD, there were also the first ever cases of bluetongue (BTV8) in the country and an incident of Highly Pathogenic Avian Influenza (H5N1). However, it is recognised that resourcing the increased requirements for patrolling, surveillance, and tracing during large or geographically dispersed outbreaks will always be the major challenge since there is a finite pool of veterinary and technical staff within Government and operational partner networks. As such, Animal Health is taking measures to ensure their plans are flexible and scalable. These measures include a re-assessment of the disease outbreak resource model, a review of roles and responsibilities of key positions, the options for centralisation of some functions, and a review of potential external resource pools and partnerships. Although the review is ongoing some of

the key features such as the use of Forward Operations Bases have already been incorporated into the latest version of the Plan.

18. Scalability will also be improved when the Animal Health Business Reform Programme (BRP) and associated IT systems are fully implemented, as reliance on relatively less stable legacy systems not suited to handling large amounts of data, will be much reduced. The aim is to have this completed by 2011. Incorporated with the issue of scalability, is the degree of decision making that can be devolved to the Local Disease Control Centres where local knowledge is used in risk assessments and to guide control options.

19. It is Defra's aim to devolve more decisions to a local level. Defra agrees there are benefits to be derived from properly defined and delineated local decision making which supports highly effective, properly focused action and make the most sensible use of resources available. Unlike other civil emergencies such as flooding, outbreaks of exotic animal disease can have widespread and national consequences. The Animal Health Agency and Defra are working together with their local operational partners to explore scenarios ranging from an isolated local incident to a large scale one that crosses borders within GB and the implications decisions can have for the resumption of trade and regaining disease freedom under international rules. They are taking into account the obligations on the UK under EU animal health legislation – including responsibilities placed on the Chief Veterinary Officer. The aim will be to set a level of local decision making that balances the need for consistency and coherency of the overall suite of control measures which itself benefits from contributions from industry stakeholders representing the national livestock industry. Defra aim to conclude these discussions within 2009.

Licensing

20. One of the major considerations in reacting to an outbreak is the balance between imposing the tightest movement restrictions to prevent the spread of disease, against a more proportionate regime to minimise otherwise economic and social costs. In order to allow each specific kind of animal movement to take place during an outbreak of FMD licenses must be issued by whoever has the relevant licensing power. Licences are legal documents that permit something, subject to conditions, that is otherwise banned by a statutory instrument. They must be written in terms that reflect their particular legal status. However, Defra is mindful of the need for plain English. Every effort is made to see that they are appropriate for the specific circumstances at that time, clearly written and easily understood.

21. Defra has a library of draft licences ready for a further outbreak of FMD and also for some other notifiable diseases. A number of draft licences were available in 2007. When the disease risk for any particular movement is considered to be low enough in the light of the particular outbreak to allow the issue of licences, the drafts are then available for use. The language of draft licences are periodically reviewed and always checked before they are issued. Improvements are being made on the identification and communication of trigger points for relaxing movement controls. This will support the Review's recommendations to identify more opportunity for local decisions.

Pirbright standing zone

22. Levels of awareness of the need to inspect livestock and report suspected cases of FMD are already high within the UK and particularly so in the area around Pirbright. The Pirbright site handles a number of different pathogens and the Specified Animal Pathogens Order (SAPO) exists to ensure that the risks of work with specified animal pathogens are effectively managed. SAPO is now enforced by the Health and Safety Executive (HSE), which is a technically competent independent authority that is actively working with IAH Pirbright to address the issues arising from its investigation in 2007[5]. Work with live animal pathogens has been restricted to a small number of sites within Pirbright where HSE and Defra are satisfied that the rigorous standards of biosecurity and biocontainment have been achieved. Work concerning these pathogens in other parts of IAH Pirbright will not resume until those containment facilities and standard operating procedures have been inspected by HSE and incorporated into a licence issued by Defra under the Specified Animal Pathogens Order 2008.

23. If the aim of a standing zone is to detect escape of virus and infection of animals in the zone as quickly as possible before spread can take place, this will require an intensive daily programme of inspections and sampling to provide the very high levels of reassurance implied by the recommendations. This could impose unnecessary costs for all concerned.

24. It is possible to devise a different plan for intermittent surveillance within the zone, but this can only provide much lower levels of reassurance which themselves could be easily offset by the false sense of security engendered. It is arguable if this would provide any greater speed of detection of escaped virus than the current measures.

25. Given the impact of surveillance in a standing zone, high cost, and the limited additional risk management gained (given that most risk would be managed by SAPO, enforced by HSE), the benefits of any incremental reduction in risk gained are far outweighed by the disproportionate cost and impact on farmers incurred, with some adverse side effects of false sense of security. This conclusion is in line with the advice of the Biosecurity Standards Group of the Office Internationale des Epizooties (OIE), and the Biological Standards Commission.

26. There is scope for targeting an enhanced awareness and education campaign aimed at livestock keepers in the area, which needs to be delivered through Animal Health Agency, local industry representatives, and other groups. This should be accompanied by a detailed analysis of the type and quality of livestock husbandry on enterprises within a 20 Kilometre radius of the Pirbright site, to achieve greater focus of effort where this is needed. Defra is considering who is best placed to deliver this work, and its conclusions will be used to inform the overall communications strategy.

---

5 Health and Safety Executive – Final report on potential breaches of biosecurity at the Pirbright site 2007

Lesson learned: Reacting with speed and certainty

Progress on lesson learned

The Review notes the contribution made by stakeholders and officials at all levels towards the critical importance of speed, including the sense of leadership and effective central control of COBR crisis management, and the rapid ramping up of effort on the ground.

The Government agrees that well-rehearsed crisis management procedures are critical to certainty and speed of response if incidents of exotic animal disease are to be contained and their impact on the economy and wider society minimised. As seen since 2001, every disease outbreak will have features unique to it. Nevertheless as Government has shown, it is possible to plan for many eventualities. As set out in the previous section, the Government will continue to rehearse and test its response to outbreaks and build up a library of licences.

Government will continue to apply the lessons learned from 2007 to giving advance notice of when domestic movement restrictions will be relaxed to enable those impacted by the restriction to better plan with speed and certainty for the impact on their businesses. With respect to speeding up our response to changes in international trade restrictions, Defra will make full use of the newly formed UK Export Certification Partnership (UKECP), a new partnership between Defra and the livestock export industry that aims to help exporters enjoy a larger share of the global market.

Review conclusions and recommendations

27. The Review concluded that all those involved in handling the 2007 FMD outbreak recognised the critical importance of speed. The speed of response during Phase 1 of the outbreak *'made a significant contribution to the overall containment'*, and Phase 2 saw an even greater level of speed and certainty in response. The speed of operations in areas such as culling, preparedness to vaccinate, and the provision of scientific support had greatly improved since the lessons learned of 2001. There was also the sense of leadership and central control at political and veterinary levels, and the COBR crisis management mechanism worked well. However, the Review recommends that more can be done to gather sound data on which to make more confident decisions.

Working in partnership

28. Animal Health is committed to partnership working and works closely with other organisations to ensure a joined up multi-agency response at the time of an outbreak. Where appropriate these organisations have representatives in the LDCC itself. Where this is not possible Animal Health is improving lines of communication to ensure they are kept briefed and informed of developments. Typically the following organisations would be involved at a local level during an outbreak of FMD in England:

- Local Authority – Animal Health and Welfare teams
- Regional and/or Local Resilience Forums / Strategic Co-ordinating Groups
- Government Office – Regional Resilience Teams
- National Farmers' Union (NFU) and other farm business representative organisations
- Police
- Environment Agency
- The vaccination contractor
- Natural England
- Military – Joint Regional Liaison Officer

29. Speed and certainty of response relies heavily on all other aspects of contingency planning such as being well prepared, practised, and in possession of a sound legislative framework. All of these aspects are discussed in further detail within this response.

Lessons learned: Communication and local knowledge

Progress on lessons learned

Defra and the Animal Health Agency recognise that good communications are crucial in maintaining stakeholder confidence during an outbreak situation. The variety of communication channels used by Defra and the Animal Health Agency during the 2007 FMD outbreak demonstrates how the Government is keen to embrace the latest technology as part of its contingency planning. Defra and the Animal Health Agency are committed to developing a wide variety of channels appropriate for the intended audience, including the website, SMS services, voicemail and direct mail. Feedback from livestock keepers in submissions to the Review was positive but some deficiencies were identified, especially on the engagement of local media. A specific role within the Defra Press Office has now been created to liaise directly with local media, as well as regular press briefings for local journalists to be held at LDCCs during an outbreak.

The importance of local knowledge in informing how Government manages an exotic disease outbreak is well recognised and incorporated within Defra's contingency planning.

Defra and Animal Health are committed to improving their engagement with Government Offices in the Regions, LACORS, local delivery partners and Local Resilience Forums, to see where their input and/or resources may be incorporated into the response plan.

Defra and Animal Health Agency will continue to develop open and transparent lines of communication with the Devolved Administrations, and to align animal health and welfare policy where possible in recognition that Great Britain is a single epidemiological unit.

Review conclusions and recommendations

30. The Review was broadly positive about Defra's outbreak communications, and recognised that lessons had been learned since 2001 and that a well-prepared framework had been put in place. The Review challenges Defra to continue to develop the channels it has available for communicating with farmers and stakeholders, paying particular attention to engaging them at a local level, in plain English. Local media, such as local radio, also needs to be engaged. The Review questions whether the current communication structure could be scaled for a larger outbreak, and suggests the possibility of developing a '*tailor-made disease emergency website*'.

31. The Review notes that Government has become more sensitive to the local and regional aspects of an exotic disease outbreak. The creation of a Core Group closely involved in decision making was an important step towards responsibility sharing, and the role of the Core Group should be reinforced and formalised. The Review recommends that Animal Health and its local managers pay greater attention to

building relationships with key local stakeholders such as local authorities and Regional Resilience Teams. Defra and Animal Health should also urgently address the animal health concordats with the Devolved Administrations, and the devolved contingency plans should be revised and updated.

Communication channels

32. The 2007 outbreak utilised more communication channels than ever before. Praise for the speed and content of the phase one communications can be found in many of the submissions made to the Review. However, by the second phase of the outbreak, the volume of communications required, as well as the emergence of Bluetongue virus, meant that certain channels became overloaded with information, and target audiences, particularly local media, began to learn of events second hand.

33. Animal Health used a wide range of communication methods during the outbreak:

    - voicemail messages to all known livestock keepers within a restricted area;
    - direct-mail information pack (often hand-delivered within a Protection Zone and Surveillance Zone) to all known livestock keepers within a control zone;
    - notification of all veterinary practices (GB-wide) of an outbreak (by means of a text message, fax or voicemail message);
    - a recorded voice information line giving headline news and advice – particularly aimed at those with limited internet access; and
    - establishment and maintenance of a local helpline.

34. Animal Health is committed to further improving communications, particularly at the local level, and will continue to look for new and innovative ways of doing this.

35. One of these innovations has been the introduction of Animal Health's free news alert subscription service, which is used to notify subscribers of latest disease outbreak news via email, fax, voicemail or SMS. This is in addition to the Poultry Register, which also has an SMS capability and will be used in the event of a poultry disease. An Animal Health recorded information line (0844 88 44 600) was also introduced during 2007. Both Animal Health and Defra continue to improve their understanding of how best to communicate with farmers and livestock keepers, based on research into channels they want Government to use during an animal disease outbreak.

36. FMD 2007 saw a step change improvement in the Defra website from 2001, and Defra is currently planning further improvements to the website navigation. This builds upon a considerable amount of user research and evaluation of current trends of usage, and is expected to deliver changes to the site structure and navigation in 2009. There are Defra-managed channels on the Directgov[6] and Business Link[7] websites and the department can make use of these resources to communicate key information to the general public and business as appropriate in the event of an emergency.

---

6   www.direct.gov.uk
7   www.businesslink.gov.uk

37. In terms of liaising with local media, the Communications Directorate at Defra identified a gap in their contingency planning and instituted a daily regional teleconference call, which increased to twice a day during the height of the outbreak. Defra have now included in their contingency planning:

   - a dedicated role within the Press Office to liaise directly with Central Office of Information News and PR (COI, formerly the Government News Network) and local media;
   - regular press briefings for local journalists held at the Local Disease Control Centre during an outbreak with the Regional Operations Director, Regional Policy Adviser and Divisional Veterinary Manager, sometimes supported by the National Farmers' Union;
   - close liaison with local authorities' and police press offices; and
   - plans for visits by regional ministers and the Chief Veterinary Officer to include briefing local media.

38. The Communications Directorate has and will continue to participate in exercises with COI News and PR and Animal Health throughout 2009, and resources permitting, run additional training sessions for COI News and PR staff on improving engagement between them, Defra, and Animal Health during a disease outbreak.

Respecting local knowledge

39. It is important to respect and utilise local knowledge in the management of a disease outbreak. The Review recommends that Animal Health pay greater attention to building relationships with key stakeholders such as local authorities, Government Offices (GOs) in the Regions, as well as Local and Regional Resilience Forums. Both Defra and Animal Health have well established links with GOs but as part of the review of local and regional preparedness, Defra and Animal Health have had discussions with the Cabinet Office, Regional Resilience Teams and Regional and Local Resilience Forums. The discussions have centred around how the animal disease control response can be better aligned with the standard emergency response mechanisms required for consequence management and in particular the role of Regional Resilience Teams and local Strategic Co-ordinating Groups (SCGs). During 2009 Animal Health will continue to build on its existing and well established links to these organisations and will undertake an analysis of local partners and stakeholders to produce an engagement plan ensuring stronger relationships with these bodies and a clearer understanding of local roles, responsibilities and communication channels in an outbreak. This will include regular formalised contact with Government Office Regional Resilience Teams and with regional and local resilience forums to share experience and knowledge of disease outbreak response. The Defra Contingency Plan has been amended to better reflect the role of SCGs and LRFs. Key stakeholders and operational partners will continue to be invited to take part in Animal Health's local exercise programme.

Case study: the partnership vision

Core Groups were established to allow Government and stakeholders to reach decisions on animal disease policy and controls by mutual consent and contribute to joint policy-development. Members of Core Groups are selected for their knowledge of particular sectors and their standing with wider stakeholder organisations, but not as representatives of particular organisations. Members of Core Groups are not generally paid for their attendance at meetings.

This relies on both sides committing to close working and frank sharing of information. In order to safeguard this, points made in core group meetings are not attributed to individual members.

Core Groups are given access to as much information on current situations, expert views and risk assessments as possible by Government. This equips them to give advice on favoured approaches and responses (including to Ministers).

The objective in all cases is to ensure that government reaches decisions which the Core Group is able to inform, endorse, support, and advocate with wider industry. That objective may not be attainable in all cases but where it is not attained the evidence base on which the parties have reached their respective views needs to be clear and the reasons for disagreement should be clearly understood in a way that maintains the mutual respect of the members for each other and for the Core Group process.

Under current legislative and constitutional arrangements the responsibility for decision making rests with Government and it is Defra which is accountable to Parliament and others for the consequences of the decisions. The normal aim therefore is that the Core Group enables government to reach decisions which have the full benefit of Core Group participation and support but which are legally the decisions of government.

It is hoped and expected that this way of working provides a valuable basis for further steps on responsibility sharing between Government and stakeholders.

Animal health concordats

40. The Review recommends that devolution issues concerning animal health be urgently addressed. The animal health concordats (which set out how the UK Government will work with the Devolved Administrations) as well as specific issues such as disease compensation are out of date. The Government agrees with the Review's conclusions that this did not cause any major problems responding to the first phase of the outbreak, but a larger outbreak or one straddling a border with England, could stretch the current arrangements. Defra currently provides funding for the delivery of animal health and welfare policy across GB through the Animal Health Agency and other delivery agents such as local authorities, even though responsibility for the policy making has been devolved.

41. Defra and the Devolved Administrations are committed to reviewing and updating concordats to a timeline that allows decisions on budgetary responsibility and other wider issues to be fully considered and agreed. Defra and the Devolved Administrations all share the view that these wider issues must not get in the way of clear lines of communication and a strong understanding of respective responsibilities in the event of an outbreak.

42. Since 2007 Defra have developed and refined mechanisms for discussion, co-ordination, and agreement of policies and disease control measures. Defra and the Devolved Administrations will use a number of informal and formal forums, including Experts Groups, regular strategic stock-takes of the Chief Veterinary Officers (UK and devolved) and regular meetings of the Animal Disease Policy Group to develop policy and co-ordinate advice to Ministers. Defra also use established methods for agreeing the UK position in international negotiations on policy and disease control measures and embed staff from the Devolved Administrations in Defra and vice versa to improve joint working in an outbreak. Defra and the Devolved Administrations have also agreed how to better co-ordinate our response in the face of an outbreak.

Lessons learned: Risk Assessment, Escalation and Management, Cost Benefit Analysis and Data

Progress on lessons learned

The Government welcomes the recognition that Defra and Animal Health showed a far greater appreciation of risk and its importance in effective disease management compared to 2001.

The Government recognises that preparedness for animal disease outbreaks is an important component of the nation's resilience to emergencies. High-level information on animal disease risks is now available in the national risk register[8] which was prepared as a consequence of the UK's national security strategy (in March 2008).

Defra has implemented an ambitious change programme to improve its capability and performance. There is a corporate management framework which supports the monitoring of progress against the Department's strategic objectives (DSOs). The Department's exotic disease policy responsibilities have been brigaded into programmes and projects with clear accountabilities to a Senior Responsible Owner (SRO). This entails having effective risk management and assurance scrutiny processes in place. The Defra Management Board holds the SROs to account. Defra will continue to put in place an increased level of challenge to help ensure that exotic animal disease policy decisions are based on good evidence and sound science and that our implementation processes are robust.

The Government is committed to seeing further improvement of risk management, particularly in areas where the assessment of likelihood and impact carry high levels of uncertainty. To help with this, in October 2008, Defra established a collaborative centre for understanding and managing environmental risks.

A new Veterinary Risk Group is being established, which will be chaired by the Government's Deputy Chief Veterinary Officer. The group will regularly monitor and rank risk across the animal health landscape, and escalate risks for action.

The Government acted quickly to implement the Callaghan Review and transferred to the Health and Safety Executive in April responsibility for the inspection and enforcement of standards at laboratories handling specified animal pathogens.

The Government recognises that the issues concerning reform of animal data systems are complex; not least because of the number and variety of customers for the data and the dependencies for the operation of systems managing CAP payments as well as animal health work. A review is currently under way to identify cost effective ways of achieving a clearer and more accurate understanding of the physical location of stock.

---

8   http://www.cabinetoffice.gov.uk/reports/national_risk_register.aspx

Review conclusions and recommendations

43. The Review acknowledged that there has been progress in the area of risk management since the 2001 outbreak. Policy decisions during the 2007 outbreak were largely based on risk assessments but there could have been more explicit consideration of the costs of control measures to the food chain. The Review recommended a more rigorous cost-benefit analysis model should be developed to address this, including an investigation into developing a more regionalised approach to disease management, in conjunction with the European Commission and Devolved Administrations.

44. The Review found that Defra's data management and information systems had not improved since 2001, and stressed that this should remain a high priority for the department.

Risk management

45. Defra is responsible for dealing with two broad categories of risk: risks to the public and the wider national interest, and risks to delivering its own business.

46. There are a number of well established risk identification mechanisms, including international disease surveillance to monitor the disease situation worldwide with a view to identifying any significant incursion of disease to new areas of the world or longer term trends in levels of distribution of disease. Qualitative risk assessments are carried out to estimate the likelihood of the disease entering the UK, and regularly published on the Defra website. Also, there is a well established cross-governmental network to identify and assess public health threats arising from potentially zoonotic diseases.

47. In order to enhance our ability to objectively prioritise and escalate risks within Defra, a new Veterinary Risk Group is to be established to regularly monitor and rank risk across the animal health landscape. Criteria will be established for appropriate responses to different types of threat. This group will make recommendations to the CVO and the relevant Senior Responsible Owners (SROs) for taking action against emerging threats. The CVO and SROs will then make the decision whether to escalate the risk or vulnerability to Defra's Management Board, with appropriate assessments of resources required to manage the risk through appropriate responses. This process is illustrated in the diagram on page 22.

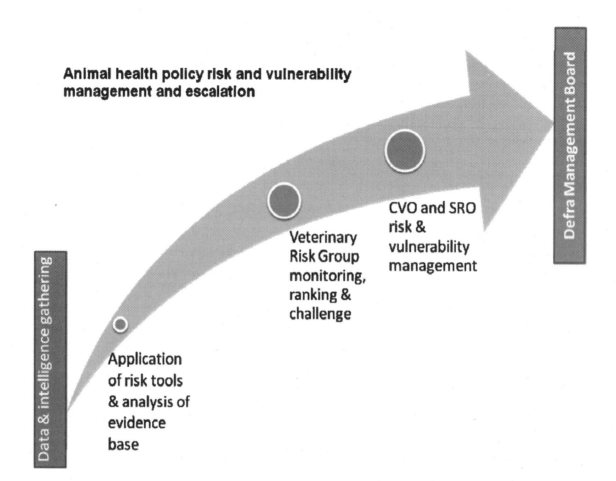

Animal health policy risk and vulnerability management and escalation

Data & intelligence gathering

Application of risk tools & analysis of evidence base

Veterinary Risk Group monitoring, ranking & challenge

CVO and SRO risk & vulnerability management

Defra Management Board

48. Defra's internal capability to carry out veterinary risk assessment is being enhanced through training programmes, and a disease modelling strategy is being developed. Both are being taken forward with the involvement of economists, since the assessment of veterinary and economic risks needs to be integrated in making policy decisions. Alongside this Defra is also carrying out a review of the risk pathways by which notifiable exotic disease could enter and spread within GB to cause an outbreak. The project will review our current understanding of the pathways of highest risk and assess the effectiveness of current control and mitigation measures. This will lead to an assessment of potential vulnerabilities which will direct the management and monitoring of exotic disease risks by setting the direction for future activities and enabling resources to be aligned to risk. A number of innovations are also being implemented at a wider departmental level, which will deliver a more consistent and robust approach to risk identification and management. For example, a common approach to policy development has been defined and disseminated. This is designed to increase the likelihood of successful policy delivery. This 'policy cycle' approach is underpinned by approval panels which oversee the release of resources for new work or for existing work that is requesting to move into a new phase of development or delivery. The panels can stop or scale down activities when resources need to be diverted to other higher priority work. A new approach to policy and project assurance is being piloted in association with the policy cycle. This requires Senior Responsible Owners (SROs) to agree the types of external scrutiny and internal peer review that their programme or project will experience.

49. A revised corporate performance management framework has been introduced. This supports the monitoring of progress in delivering the Department's strategic objectives (DSOs) and in living within its means. The Management Board now receives regular progress reports from Director-level SROs on both DSOs and selected high-risk programmes. Most of Defra's work is now brigaded into programmes and projects, with clear accountabilities, and this is allowing senior managers to manage the Department's work as a portfolio.

50. In October 2008, Defra established a collaborative centre for understanding and managing environmental risks. The Centre is led by Professor Simon Pollard from Cranfield University (who is Professor of Environmental Risk Management and who participated in Sir John Beringer's review of the Institute of Animal Health). The impetus for the Centre came partly from criticism by Defra's Science Advisory Council, which recommended that Defra needed a system of risk appraisal that is transparent, acknowledges uncertainty, and encompasses an appropriately wide range of techniques. The Centre establishes a three-year partnership with Cranfield, with the express aim of helping the Department to improve the quality of the evidence that Defra uses to assess and compare the risks across its diverse portfolio. Three other co-funders are involved in this collaboration: the Natural Environment Research Council, the Economics and Social Research Council, and the Engineering and Physical Sciences Research Council.

51. The Management Board specifically relies on its Audit and Risk Committee (ARC) (with its non-executive chair and non-executive members) to systematically look at risk management and escalation in the Department, and to flag up any generic weaknesses or concerns. This role involves reviewing key information on Defra's risk, governance and control environment on an ongoing basis – supported by information from Internal Audit – and discussing key issues with senior policy and delivery managers, and with the chairs of the audit committees across the Defra network.

52. As with other departments, Defra's Accounting Officer (the Permanent Secretary) publishes an annual statement on the Department's internal control (SIC)[9]. This statement accompanies the publication of the Department's resource accounts and includes required sections which comment on Defra's capacity to handle risk, the risk and control framework, the effectiveness of risk management, and any significant control issues.

53. The ARC is mindful of the concerns raised by the Review, and its forward agenda will investigate how risks are managed and monitored at the policy:delivery interface and how the Department's new performance management system is working, including the escalation of risk.

---

9   http://www.defra.gov.uk/corporate/finance/resource-accounts/accounts0708/resourceaccounts-0708. pdf#page=35.

54. The combination of work to improve the management of risk at a wider corporate level in Defra and the specific improvement activities to prioritise risks and identify vulnerabilities in the animal disease policy area should provide the senior team in the Food and Farming Group and Defra's Management Board with a more coherent picture of the Department's portfolio of animal disease related risks. This then holds out an improved opportunity to allocate resources on the basis of risk.

Cost Benefit Analysis

55. Sound cost-benefit analysis enables the pros and cons of different courses of action to be weighed – for example, balancing the costs and social impacts of retaining animal movement controls against any potential gain arising from earlier relaxation of export restrictions. As well as appraising the costs and benefits, sound economic analysis also incorporates the effects of incentives and behavioural responses which are essential to consider when assessing disease control measures.

56. Defra has increased its capacity for economic analysis (including cost benefit analysis of disease control) with an additional senior economist. In addition, it will:

   • establish a framework for undertaking relevant economic analysis in an outbreak, building on existing epidemiological and economic model capacity, and taking account of the likely key decision points
   • refine its ability to model down-stream impacts of disease outbreaks and movement restrictions – in particular, with further analysis of markets and to assist consideration by industry on the merits or otherwise of introducing change to their structure and operations.

57. Recognising that analytical capacity is only one element of improving economic input into policy-making, we will also:

   • formalise the ways in which economic advice comes into decision-making by creating a clear route of advice on economic analysis and industry intelligence into Minsters and the Animal Disease Policy Group
   • build capacity of policy-makers in understanding the place of economic advice in disease control decisions.

Data

58. The issues concerning reform of animal data systems are complex but Defra acknowledges that progress has been slower than anticipated. Significant investment has however taken place since 2001. As a result of £21 million investment in the Cattle Tracing System (CTS) electronic channels to report births and movements now account for around 70% of all birth and movement transactions. Electronic notifications are faster and more accurate than paper, and have resulted in a huge improvement in data quality on CTS over the past few years. Movement anomalies have decreased from a peak of 1.2 million in 2003 to around 220,000 today.

59. The system that was unavailable for a short period during the 2007 FMD outbreak was not CTS as stated in the Anderson Review but a management information system that is generally very reliable. Some urgent reports of animals on location therefore had to be produced manually, resulting in poorer accuracy than would otherwise have been the case.

60. The Animal Movements Licensing System was developed as part of the FMD recovery plan in 2002. It too was upgraded and enhanced in 2005 (at a cost of £950,000). This has improved the flexibility and reliability of the system.

61. A new analytical system, RADAR (Rapid Analysis and Detection of Animal-related Risks) has also been developed. This system draws the restricted areas at the outset of an outbreak and analyses the animal movement data (from CTS and AMLS) to provide an initial estimate of which other parts of the country may be affected by disease and which areas are probably free. It allows surveillance and tracing visits to be prioritised according to risk and some areas of the country to be lifted out of restriction more quickly or to avoid them all together. It has delivered a step change in evidence-based decision making and has a fully integrated GIS component (capable of visualising the Rural Payments Agency Land Register data) which is used to supply all the maps to the National Disease Control Centre and COBR.

62. The quality of data provided to CTS and AMLS is as critical as the systems themselves. Defra recognises the need for reform of its location identifiers, to give a clearer and more accurate understanding of the actual physical location of stock. An underlying issue is that of the accuracy and usability of the location identifier within the systems. A review is currently under way to identify as a matter of urgency cost effective ways of achieving this outcome.

Lesson learned: The Legislative Framework

Progress on lesson learned

The Government welcomes Sir Iain's recognition that the Government took seriously his 2002 recommendations and found that Government had acted quickly to tackle the shortcomings he had identified. He has not identified any new lessons to learn in this section of his report.

Nevertheless it is understood that the legislative framework needs to be kept under review to ensure it is reflecting lessons learned from new outbreaks and is flexible to adapt to future challenges.

Review conclusions and recommendations

63. The Review recognised that the shortcomings in legislation identified from the 2001 FMD outbreak had been overcome, and that the legislative framework has been strengthened. Moreover, the Review concluded that all the legislative changes that have been made were critical in responding effectively to the 2007 outbreak. Incorporated with legislation is the subject of licensing.

FMD Order 2006

64. The FMD Directive[10] was agreed in 2003 and amended the previous EU legislation for the control and eradication of FMD, taking account of the most recent scientific developments in the field of disease control; the experience gained in eradicating FMD during the 2001 outbreak, and technical developments in laboratory diagnosis of FMD and vaccines. In particular, the Directive moved emergency vaccination to the forefront of FMD control strategies, alongside the basic slaughter policy, and required member states to have detailed plans for emergency vaccination in their contingency plans.

65. The Directive was transposed in full in England in the form of the Animal Health Act 1981 (as amended), the Foot-and-Mouth Disease (England) Order 2006[11] and the Foot-and-Mouth Disease (Control of Vaccination)(England) Regulations 2006[12] which set out the legal powers and obligations around notification, suspicion and investigation of the disease; and measures following confirmation of disease. The Orders came into force in February 2006 and completely replaced the pre-existing FMD legislation.

---

10   Council Directive 2003/85/EC
11   Statutory Instrument 2006 No.182 The Foot-and-Mouth Disease (England) Order 2006
12   Statutory Instrument 2006 No.183 The Foot-and-Mouth Disease (Control of Vaccination)(England) Regulations 2006

Animal Health Act 1981 and 2002

66. Under the Animal Health Act 1981 (as amended in 2002) Defra is required to publish a national contingency plan. The plan is reviewed annually and, where revision is necessary, updated to reflect our latest experiences. It is subject to extensive public consultation before being laid before Parliament. The plan sets out in detail the structure, roles and responsibilities involved in disease control so that there is absolute clarity about what needs to be done and by whom. The plan consists of the Defra Framework Response Plan and a separate document, Defra's Overview of Emergency Preparedness which sets out details of the operational capacity to support the Response Plan including arrangements for culling and disposal and the large number of contingency contracts which are in place. The 2008 version of these documents were laid before Parliament last December, and were available on the Defra website[13]. The new versions take account of the lessons Government have learnt from the 2007 FMD outbreak, other recent incidences of exotic notifiable disease and the responses from the recent public consultation. A summary of the main changes are also available on the Defra website.

67. The Act also clarifies the preventive slaughter powers and creates a duty to consider vaccination and to publish reasons for not using vaccination if a contiguous cull was used.

Civil Contingencies Act 2004

68. The Civil Contingencies Act 2004 provides legal powers to respond to emergencies, including animal health emergencies, and establishes a new statutory framework for civil protection planning at the local level using Local Resilience Forums. The emergency response powers contained within the Act have not been required for any exotic animal disease outbreak to-date and were not required in 2007.

Working with the European Union / Standing Committee on the Food Chain and Animal Health

69. Throughout the outbreak the Commission was kept abreast of developments as and when they occurred. Over the course of the outbreak, Defra wrote to the Commission 24 times, provided 10 detailed weekly reports, and gave 5 presentations to the Standing Committee on the Food Chain and Animal Health (SCoFCAH).

70. As a result, the relationship with the Commission was positive. The Commission was helpful and satisfied with the action that Defra had taken. The EU safeguard measures affecting exports and imports were adapted to reflect the developing disease situation.

71. The Review recommended that the Government should work with the Commission and Member States to look again at the wider trade implications of restrictions on export of animal bi-products. By working closely with the retail sector during and since the 2007 FMD outbreak Government has become better aware of the

---

13 http://www.defra.gov.uk/animalh/diseases/control/contingency/exotic.htm

difficulties this sector faced as a result of these export restrictions, particularly where these difficulties relate to products considered to be of low risk in the transmission of disease (composite products). Both Defra and representatives of the retail sector are currently preparing proposals to present to the European Commission which would look to exempt low risk composite products from any future safeguard measures.

Regionalisation

72. Following confirmation of any exotic disease, the primary objective is to contain, and where appropriate, eradicate the disease as fast and effectively as possible and restore the UK's disease free status. In doing so Defra select control strategies which:

   - minimise the number of animals which need to be culled either to control the disease or on welfare grounds, and which keep animal welfare problems to a minimum;
   - protect public health;
   - cause the least possible disruption to the food, farming and tourism industries, to visitors to the countryside, and to rural communities in the wider economy;
   - minimise damage to the environment; and
   - minimise the burden on taxpayers and the public.

73. In handling any outbreak, Government needs to take strategic decisions to determine where the economic balance of interest lies, especially between domestic and international trade and regions with the UK (see paragraph 56 on cost benefit analysis).

74. The Review recommended that Defra, in co-operation with the EU and the Devolved Administrations, build on the experience of 2007 and further develop a regionalised and risk based approach. Details of the risk based approach taken by Defra are set out at paragraph 48.

75. Any regionalised approach to disease control would have to be in accordance with OIE (World Organisation for Animal Health) principles; three zones would be established with different levels of certainty as to their disease status:

   - A higher risk zone, out of which movements of live animals are prohibited and movements of meat are restricted.
   - A buffer zone, out of which meat may be traded provided that it is traceable to an origin outside the higher risk zone. Live animals would not be able to move out of this zone to the free zone but should be able to move into the higher risk zone for slaughter.
   - A free zone with normal movements allowed of both live animals and meat but with certification to assure importing countries that they do originate in the free zone.

76. The three most important factors in determining the size of these zones are disease control and surveillance, domestic trade, and international trade. Creating an evidence base on which to determine the size of these zones, and the trigger points that

would need to be satisfied for lifting them is difficult. The large volume of information that would need to be collated could only be carried out with full commitment from industry. Even with a sound evidence base, the livestock food and retail chain is highly complex and integrated, and does not easily lend itself to a regionalised approach to disease control.

77. Defra is working with the Devolved Administrations to achieve greater clarity and understanding of the issues affecting exit strategies from the various restrictions applied in response to an exotic disease outbreak. The EU, Member States and third countries with whom Great Britain trade will be looking for assurance on how the boundaries between regions with different disease status are being policed. A cost benefit analysis will be critical given the integrated nature of much of our livestock and food production sectors. In addition, the veterinary risk assessment (VRA) processes will be strengthened and Defra is supporting work lead by the Scottish Government on updated VRAs for movement restrictions.

Lesson learned: Basing policy decisions on the best available science

Progress on lesson learned

The Review found Government positioned science at the centre of the 2007 control strategies and concluded this was a major lesson learned from 2001.

Science forms the backbone of Defra's evidence based strategy to eradicate any exotic animal disease outbreak. Building upon the lessons learnt from the 2001 outbreak Defra has ensured that the latest scientific and veterinary developments form an integral part of our disease response. The Scientific Advisory Council sub group on exotic diseases provides scientific advice to Defra's Chief Scientific Adviser as required. Both the SAC and the CSA audit and advise on the science and strategic assumptions. As brought out in this section and elsewhere in the Government's response, Defra will continue to improve its science evidence base. The CSA (or his deputy) are kept informed on a daily basis during the outbreak by the CVO's team, and through his knowledge of the external subject expertise available in SAC and beyond, the CSA can arrange for ad hoc groups to meet quickly to consider specific issues, or to challenge the validity of scientific assumptions made and their impact on control measures.

Review conclusions and recommendations

78. The Review states that Defra has recognised the need to put science at the heart of policy decision making with respect to exotic disease, and that risk assessments are now a routine part of this process. It recommends that these assessments (as well as other scientific advice) are published by Defra and the Devolved Administrations in order to strengthen wider confidence amongst stakeholders in their decisions. The Review also suggests that Defra increase the level of technical and scientific expertise at hand, both outside and during times of disease outbreak. This should also aid Defra in continuing to drive the debate surrounding vaccination.

Building technical and scientific expertise

79. Defra is increasing the number of veterinary advisers who can lead and contribute to formulation of veterinary risk assessments (VRAs). Training is being developed with the aim of introducing a standard methodology which will include seeking and incorporating contributions from a wide range of experts, including epidemiologists, scientists and economists (amongst others). Defra agrees that VRAs should be published on its website and will also create a library of VRAs to provide a source of reference for the future.

80. Policy development for control of exotic diseases is strongly supported by Expert Groups which are convened both during business as usual and emergencies to consider specific veterinary and science questions which need more detailed attention. Defra are currently reviewing the composition and reporting procedures for

these groups and it has been agreed that the outputs from Expert Group meetings should be published on Defra's website.

81. Additional challenges to the science and wider evidence base for exotic disease policy comes from the Science Advisory Council which reports to Defra's Chief Scientific Adviser. The SAC provides a vital critical friend role and its membership brings a large amount of external experience and insight to bear on assessing the value of the current and future evidence base. Veterinary officials meet Defra's Chief Scientific Adviser (or his deputy) regularly during outbreaks of notifiable disease, and consideration is being given to how this might be incorporated more formally into the battle rhythm established to deal with outbreaks.

Epidemiology

82. Epidemiology is the study of the causes, level, and distribution of disease, based on a careful analysis of the data and information available, and taking into account alternative explanations for apparent effects, missing data and other factors that may affect the interpretation of the data. In a disease outbreak this investigative and analytical work is delivered by the National Emergency Epidemiology Group (NEEG) whose core is formed by the Epidemiology Group within the Veterinary Science team in Defra. This Group is expanded in a disease outbreak to become the NEEG, which comprises post-graduate level trained veterinary epidemiologists supported by information management specialists from Defra and VLA, and Animal Health Veterinary Officers who have received additional 'short course' training in epidemiology who carry out field investigations. The NEEG also has a working arrangement with a number of academic modelling groups who provide analyses that help to predict the future course of the outbreak and how different control measures may affect this. All of these investigations are collated to provide a picture of where disease is and so guide the choice and application of control measures. The NEEG also uses its expertise to design surveillance protocols to detect the extent to which disease may have dispersed, to monitor the effect of the controls, and to give advice on progress towards eradication.

Veterinary Training and Research Initiative (VTRI)

83. Following the FMD outbreak in 2001 Defra funded a significant initiative – The Veterinary Training and Research Initiative – to support research and education in the area of population medicine and disease control. Liverpool Veterinary School's intercalated MSc programme has graduated about 10 students per year who go on to complete their veterinary clinical training and graduate with specific skills in disease control and a basis in epidemiology. Defra has further supplemented this training by providing internship posts for these students since 2007 as well as offering research project opportunities which are more closely linked to key policy areas. This initiative provides the opportunity to bring younger vets into the government service better equipped with a stronger skill set to move into state veterinary medicine, including epidemiology. However, numbers remain small. Although the benefits will take some time to evaluate, the quality of interns working in Defra provides strong evidence of their potential to make key contribution to public roles in the future.

RCVS Modular Certificate

84. Other initiatives to improve the veterinary skill set within Government includes a new RCVS post-graduate modular certificate, that includes public sector specific modules addressing epidemiology, international animal health, disease control, animal welfare, and public health in relation both to food assurance and zoonoses.

85. The RCVS subcommittee has also now endorsed a new named certificate in Epidemiology. Defra are currently working with the key University epidemiology groups, notably the RVC, Liverpool and Glasgow to implement the RCVS Certificate in Epidemiology.

In-house training

86. Defra's Veterinary Science Team is currently working with the Royal Veterinary College and colleagues in other member states to develop training and effective methods for implementing Veterinary Risk Assessment work within policy environments.

87. A pilot training session run by Defra with input from colleagues from Denmark and Serbia took place in October 2008. All newly appointed Veterinary Advisors and some colleagues from Animal Health have commenced this training.

Delivering Research and Innovation through Veterinary Expertise (DRIVE)

88. A new project in development known as DRIVE (*Delivering Research and Innovation through Veterinary Expertise*), aims to provide a strategic approach to veterinary resource across government in the future. This strategy is in-line with the Cabinet Office initiative to expand the role of the Heads of Profession across government to more effectively advise them on workforce planning issues as well as skills and expertise demands.

Sir Iain Anderson's Personal Recommendations

89. Sir Iain Anderson, in the foreword of the Review, makes two personal recommendations. The first includes the recommendation to reposition the Institute of Animal Health (IAH) as a new National Institute of Infectious Diseases.

90. Defra, DIUS and BBSRC have discussed over the past year the future facilities needed for animal health in the UK and specifically the future management and arrangements at IAH Pirbright. BBSRC will continue to fund the Institute for Animal Health so that it can provide the nation with world class research facilities that underpin the livestock industries and our food security. DIUS expect BBSRC soon to submit a business case for the redevelopment of the site at Pirbright to allow the continuation of world class research there on animal diseases. Defra will continue to work with DIUS and BBSRC to ensure that the national provision of research, diagnosis and surveillance enables effective disease detection and response. The Institute for Animal Health and the Veterinary Laboratories Agency will continue to pursue opportunities for collaboration.

91. The second personal recommendation concerns the creation of a new **independent advisory committee**. Defra believes that existing groups and committees fulfil this function. There are three key independent expert advisory groups that provide advice to Ministers, the Chief Medical Officer, the Chief Veterinary Officer, and the Health and Safety Executive on the risks to animal and human health and safety from exposure to pathogens, particularly those that are zoonotic:-

    - The Advisory Committee on Dangerous Pathogens
    - Advisory Committee on Microbiological Safety of Food
    - National Expert Panel on New and Emerging Infections.

92. These groups also join officials across Government and relevant agencies in risk assessment and management. The Panel also joins all the Chairs of other expert advisory committees, such as SEAC, in addressing potential risks to the UK from infectious diseases. In addition to these, the UK Zoonoses, Animal Diseases and Infections Group of senior Government Officials is chaired in rotation by CVOs and CMOs and ensures an integrated, multi-disciplinary and cross-government approach to risk management policy on these infections.

93. At a working level, the Human Animal Infection and Risk Group provides ongoing assessment of the zoonotic potential of emerging infectious hazards and feeds into the Panel and the UK Zoonoses, Animal Diseases and Infections Group. In addition, a subgroup of Defra's independent Science Advisory Council also provides ad hoc advice on scientific aspects of specific epidemic disease issues.

ANNEX: Response to individual recommendations

LESSON	Ref	RECOMMENDATION	RESPONSE
Maintain vigilance	R1	We recommend that Defra work with the new UK Border Agency to ensure that vigilance is maintained, and where possible, strengthened.	**Accept.** Defra will continue to work with the UKBA just as it has done with HMRC since 2003. Discussions on the exact scope of roles and responsibilities are still ongoing between HMRC and UKBA but the current level of resources allocated to Products Of Animal Origin (POAO) enforcement activities will be maintained. Defra will undertake further work on risk with HMRC/UKBA to ensure that their enforcement efforts are targeted to where there is the greatest risk. Defra/HMRC and the UKBA will maintain ongoing public awareness campaigns in the UK and abroad as part of a joint publicity strategy. Defra will continue to work with Animal Health/Local Authorities and HMRC/the new UKBA to ensure compliance with EU and GB rules for the commercial importation of live animals and POAO from outside the EU, through Border Inspection Posts. Defra will continue to work at EU and international level to influence other EU member states and third countries and minimise the risk of introducing disease into the UK.
	R2	We recommend that Defra consider the case for a standing zone around Pirbright with higher levels of surveillance and greater awareness-raising of the potential risks.	**Accept.** Defra has fully considered the case for a standing zone. The level of surveillance implied by the Anderson Review would impose a highly significant impact on all concerned, including businesses in the zone as well as for Animal Health Agency resources and costs to the exchequer. Defra questions the benefits of this given the measures put in place to improve risk management at the site. They include a new operational agreement between the Institute of Animal Health and Merial on roles and responsibilities and the transfer of responsibility for inspection and enforcement of standards to the Health and Safety Executive. Defra agrees that it is important to maintain high levels of awareness. However this is not just an issue for livestock keepers in the vicinity of Pirbright. It is a key point for all livestock keepers given the range of exotic diseases and the unquantifiable potential for incursion of diseases and the subsequent infection of livestock. The Government therefore intends to continue to work with the veterinary profession and industry leaders to ensure that all livestock keepers understand their obligations relating to regular inspection of livestock, being aware of the commonly expected clinical signs of the relevant notifiable diseases, and also of the need to report suspicion of disease as quickly as possible and knowing how to do so.

LESSON	Ref	RECOMMENDATION	RESPONSE
Be prepared	R3	We recommend that Defra place greater emphasis on testing the full emergency response chain, involving critical contractors and operational partners.	**Accept.** Animal Health will ensure that all elements of the emergency response chain are tested as part of their established exercise programme. The 2008/9 programme focuses on critical control points and includes key contingency contracts and operational partners. Key operational partners, such as local authorities, are already routinely involved in the existing local exercise programme. We will have rehearsed two key contingency contracts by end of January 2009 with further exercises planned to test the establishment of Forward Operations Bases, the transport of equipment, and the deployment of labour and cleansing and disinfection equipment planned for later in 2009. There will be a national exercise across Government Departments in 2010.
	R4	We recommend that there be a fundamental overhaul of the arrangements for selecting, training, deploying and rewarding the Regional Operations Directors (RODs) and Divisional Operations Managers (DOMs).	**Accept.** Animal Health is undertaking a critical review of the Government's outbreak response model in liaison with Defra and the Devolved Administrations. This includes a reassessment of job roles in both the National and Local Disease Control Centres of which Regional Operations Directors (RODs) and Divisional Operations Managers (DOMs) are key. The revised job roles along with the new role of Regional Policy Adviser have been included in the latest version of the Defra Contingency Plan which was laid before Parliament in December 2008. These changes will significantly increase the pool from which these key appointments can be made. Changes have also been made to the remuneration arrangements to make the ROD role more attractive.
	R5	We recommend that Animal Health review the skills, experience and general level of preparedness of their staff in key skills such as data handling.	**Accept.** Animal Health continually reviews the Government's outbreak response model in liaison with Defra and the Devolved Administrations. Recently attention has focused on an assessment of the key skills and competencies required in Disease Control Centres. Animal Health is introducing a skills register to assist with the deployment of appropriately trained staff in an outbreak.
	R6	We recommend that Defra review the scalability of its existing contingency plans and emergency staffing models.	**Accept.** Animal Health continually reviews the Government's outbreak response model in liaison with Defra and the Devolved Administrations. Recently this has included exploring potential external resource pools and partnerships. Some recommendations of the review – such as the use of Forward Operations Bases (FOBs) – have been included in the latest version of the Contingency Plan laid before Parliament in December 2008.
	R7	We recommend that Defra, drawing on the experience in 2007, should do more to prepare generic licences for use in a future disease outbreak, ensuring that all documents are in plain English.	**Accept.** Defra has a library of draft licences ready for a further outbreak of foot-and-mouth disease and for outbreaks of some other notifiable diseases. A number of draft FMD licences were available in 2007. To help us improve the draft licences, we are working with others with practical farming and enforcement experience in helping us improve them. Every effort is made to see that they are clearly written and easily understood. We are also looking at how we might clarify the expected trigger points for relaxing movement controls and at publishing this clarification in order that those impacted by the restrictions can better plan for them. This work is linked to a wider review of issues around timing of removal of restrictions in exotic disease outbreaks, e.g. to facilitate export trade as early as possible.

LESSON	Ref	RECOMMENDATION	RESPONSE
	R8	We recommend that Defra continues to develop and test its policies and arrangements for emergency vaccination, as a central element of its control strategy, ensuring that the full implications of vaccination are thought through and widely understood.	**Accept.** Defra and Animal Health work closely together to test all elements of the response policy and operational readiness. Animal Health is currently re-tendering the contract to deliver FMD vaccination and aims to put in place a flexible contract which will improve capability to vaccinate against other exotic diseases where that would be an appropriate response. Defra and Animal Health will continue to keep under review the science behind vaccination as a disease control strategy and vaccine technical developments; not just for FMD but also for other exotic animal diseases. This includes continuing engagement with consumer organisations, those involved in the food production chain and others about the circulation of products derived from vaccinated animals. Work will include an examination of the Cost Benefit Analyses of different vaccination strategies.
	R9	We recommend that Defra look to increase the level of decision making it is possible to delegate to those on the ground, at the LDCC, during an outbreak.	**Accept.** This requires planning against a range of scenarios and working through the issues around the international obligations of the UK and the CVO specifically. Representatives of local partners will be involved in the planning. Unlike some other emergency areas, exotic animal diseases will always have an impact on international trade and decisions to be applied locally need to be cognisant of the national and international consequences. The work to build the library of movement licences and agreement on trigger points for their use should enable more local decisions to be taken.
React with speed and certainty	R10	We recommend that the arrangements for responding to notifiable disease reports be rehearsed regularly.	**Accept.** Animal Health routinely responds to reports of notifiable disease and has an established programme of exercises in each of its Divisional Offices. Further work has been undertaken to audit the disease reporting process to build a continuous improvement and quality assurance mechanism. This includes looking at the arrangements for notifying and mounting the response delivered by other local operational partners.

LESSON	Ref	RECOMMENDATION	RESPONSE
Explain policies, plans and practices	R11	We recommend that Defra continue to develop a 'menu of communication opportunities' for use in any crisis.	**Accept.** Opportunities cover what needs to be communicated, when, how and to whom. Defra continues to improve its understanding of how best to communicate with farmers, based on research into channels they want Defra to use during an animal disease outbreak. Since 2001, Animal Health has introduced several new channels which increase the menu of communication opportunities available. Animal Health has also introduced a free subscription service for Disease Alerts, which is used to notify subscribers of latest disease outbreak news via email, fax, voicemail or SMS. This is in addition to the Poultry Register, which also has an SMS capability and will be used in the event of a poultry disease. FMD 2007 saw a step change improvement in the Defra website from 2001, and plans are in place for further improvements to the website navigation. This will be achieved through a considerable amount of user research and evaluation of current trends of usage, and is expected to deliver changes to the site structure and navigation in 2009. There are now Defra-managed "channels" on the Directgov (www.direct.gov.uk) and Business Link (www.businesslink.gov.uk) websites and we make use of these resources to communicate key information to the general public and business as appropriate in the event of an emergency.
	R12	We recommend that engagement with the local media be improved.	**Accept.** A gap identified in Defra's communication contingency planning led to the introduction of a daily regional teleconference call, which increased to twice a day during the height of the outbreak. Defra have now included in its contingency planning: • a dedicated role within the Press Office to liaise directly with COI News and PR (formerly GNN) and local media • regular press briefings for local journalists held at the Local Disease Control Centre during an outbreak with the Regional Operations Director and Divisional Veterinary Manager, sometimes supported by the NFU • close liaison with local authorities' and police press offices • plans for visits by regional ministers and the Chief Veterinary Officer to include briefing local media. The Defra Communications Directorate has participated in exercises with COI News and PR and Animal Health throughout 2008 and will continue to do so in 2009, and resources permitting, will during 2009, run additional training sessions for COI News and PR staff on improving engagement between them, Defra, and Animal Health during a disease outbreak.

LESSON	Ref	RECOMMENDATION	RESPONSE
Respect local knowledge	R13	We recommend that Animal Health and its local managers pay greater attention to building relationships with key stakeholders.	**Accept.** Animal Health understands this recommendation to refer particularly to relations with local authorities, Government Offices in the Regions and Local & Regional Resilience Forums. Animal Health is strengthening its engagement. By January 2009 we will have met with officials from the Civil Contingencies Secretariat and lead officials from the regional Government Offices and agreed an engagement plan and better arrangements for formalised contact with Government Office regional resilience teams and with LRFs to share experience and knowledge of disease outbreak response. Key operational partners will continue to be invited to take part in Animal Health's local exercise programme. Moreover, Defra policy makers are ensuring that they have stronger links into the Government Office network and Civil Contingencies Secretariat.
	R14	We recommend that devolution issues concerning animal health be urgently addressed, and that concordats be reviewed.	**Accept.** Defra and Devolved Administrations are committed to close and productive joint working on policy co-ordination for animal health policy and on disease control responses. The concordats are under review, but some of the issues that need to be resolved are complex and linked to broader developments, e. g. on responsibility and cost sharing, that will need to be worked through in detail and may take some time. Even in the absence of agreed reviewed concordats, a number of formal and informal mechanisms are in place for the co-ordination of policy and disease control, e. g. through expert groups, the Animal Disease Policy Group, and regular CVO stock-takes.
	R15	We recommend Defra reinforce and formalise the role of the Core Group in decision making as part of its move towards greater responsibility sharing.	**Accept.** The Core Group have become a tried and tested part of policy making on disease control issues. Defra is continuing to increase its work with core industry stakeholders in this way, with groups now established on bluetongue, foot and mouth, avian influenza, and classical swine fever. An equine Core Group is also being set up. The experience of working with core groups has been positive for policy-makers and Ministers and is being seen as a model for other areas of work and as a mechanism which can be further developed in line with the broader responsibility and cost sharing agenda.

LESSON	Ref	RECOMMENDATION	RESPONSE
Risk assessment and cost benefit analysis	R16	We recommend that Defra adopt a more rigorous cost benefit analysis model for disease control measures.	**Accept.** Defra has increased its capacity for economic analysis (including cost benefit analysis of disease control) with an additional senior economist. Defra will also: • Establish a framework for undertaking relevant economic analysis in an outbreak building on existing epidemiological and economic model capacity, and taking account of the likely key decision points. • Refine our ability to model down-stream impacts of disease outbreaks and movement restrictions – in particular, with further analysis of markets and to assist consideration by industry on the merits or otherwise of introducing change to their structure and operations. Recognising that economic models are only one step to improve economic input into policy-making, Defra will also: • Formalise the ways in which economic advice comes into decision-making by creating a clear route of advice on economic analysis and industry intelligence into Ministers and the Animal Disease Policy Group. • Build capacity of policy-makers in understanding the place of economic advice in disease control decisions.
	R17	We recommend that Defra agree with the EU specific exemptions from trade restrictions on highly processed products of animal origin.	**Accept.** Defra is working closely with the retail sector to better understand their issues, especially in relation to products considered to be of low risk in the transmission of disease (composite products). Both the Department and representatives of the retail sector are currently preparing proposals to present to the European Commission which would look to exempt low risk composite products from any future safeguard measures
	R18	We recommend that Defra – in co-operation with the EU and the devolved administrations – build on the experience of 2007 and further develop a regionalised and risk based approach to disease management.	**Accept.** Defra is taking forward work with the Devolved Administrations which will see greater clarity and understanding of the issues affecting exit strategies from the various restrictions applied in response to an exotic disease outbreak. A new post at Deputy Director level has been agreed to drive and co-ordinate Defra's engagement in this work. A new senior economist has been recruited to deliver improved economic analysis, including analysis of the costs and benefits of regionalising parts of GB to minimise the impact of movement restrictions. Clearly the EU and our Member State partners and third countries with whom Great Britain trade will be looking for assurance on how the boundaries between regions with different disease status would be policed. The cost benefit analysis will be critical given the integrated nature of much of our livestock and food production sectors. The veterinary risk assessment (VRA) process is being strengthened and Defra is supporting work lead by the Scottish Government on updated VRAs for movement restrictions. In addition a new post has been created at Deputy Director level to look at broader aspects of exiting from disease controls.

LESSON	Ref	RECOMMENDATION	RESPONSE
	R19	We recommend that Defra's Audit and Risk Committee should review processes within Defra for identifying and elevating risks to board level. The Committee should publish its findings.	**Accept.** Defra has completed a change programme which saw its portfolio of work brigaded into programmes and projects. This has involved raising awareness still further about good risk management. Guidance and instructions have been disseminated to staff, underpinned by training targeted at Senior Responsible Owners, programme and project managers. The role of Defra's Audit and Risk Committee (as defined in Treasury Guidance) is to support Defra's Management Board and the Accounting Officer by reviewing the assurances given to the Board in respect of risk management, governance, and internal controls. It will draw to the Board's attention any areas which it feels should be improved. The Audit and Risk Committee's (ARC) forward plan for 2009 will include a review of progress in implementing improvements in risk management. The ARC will not publish a specific report of its review, but its findings will inform the risk elements of the Department's next Statement on Internal Control which is published.
Data and information management systems	R20	We recommend that the Business Reform Programme and the associated Livestock Partnership Programme be prioritised and appropriately funded by Defra and Animal Health.	**Accept.** The Business Reform Programme (BRP) is a very high priority for Animal Health and Defra and continues to be funded accordingly. The need for a resolution to the data issues is being taken seriously and work is being done to identify a resolution as soon as possible.
	R21	We recommend that the full potential of GIS technology with all its benefits be incorporated into future data systems.	**Accept.** Defra anticipate that the data solutions referred to under R20 will accommodate appropriate interfaces with GI systems to provide the spatial information handling capability.
	R22	We recommend that the information systems interface with Genus be subject to a simulated load test, end-to-end.	**Accept.** This has been completed. Animal Health and Genus have conducted (30 April 2008) an end-to-end data exercise which simulated data exchange from the pre vaccination phase through data scheduling to the post vaccination phase. This has provided Defra, Animal Health and Genus with a significant level of reassurance and understanding to ensure systems will be able to cope with the demands placed upon them in a real outbreak. Plans are now in place to make such testing an annual event.
	R23	We recommend that Defra develop a contingency plan to secure the existing IT systems while the Business Reform Programme and Livestock Partnership Programme are being developed.	**Accept.** Steps have been taken to improve the resilience of existing IT systems through investment in hardware and software solutions. The reliance on the VetNet system in particular has been reduced by the roll out of the new customer registration and contact management system.

LESSON	Ref	RECOMMENDATION	RESPONSE
Base policy decisions on best available science	R24	We recommend that Defra increase the level of technical and scientific expertise available to contribute to the development of disease control policies on a day-to-day basis, not just during a disease outbreak.	**Accept.** This is being delivered through a number of ways. A Collaborative Centre for understanding and managing environmental risks has been established. The Epidemiology Group that has been formed in Defra since the 2007 FMD outbreak now has a complement of 4 vets trained in epidemiology to post graduate level, each of whom provides epidemiological advice on defined diseases and participates in the development of control policies, contingency plans and exercises to test those plans. Work is in hand to develop collaborative working arrangements with the VLA epidemiologists, in order to provide access to additional capability during an outbreak.
	R25	We recommend that there be greater transparency in publishing scientific advice and risk assessments.	**Accept.** A Veterinary Risk Group is being established to regularly review and update risk assessments across animal health matters. Defra is supporting work being lead by the Scottish Government on veterinary risk assessments of movement controls. The intention is to publish the VRAs produced. Defra already regularly publishes VRAs in response to changes in disease situation outside the UK.
	R26	We recommend that Defra continue to drive the vaccination debate, ensuring that all of the issues are communicated clearly and properly explained.	**Accept.** Defra continues to facilitate the vaccination debate in its discussions with stakeholder organisations, including consumers and those along the food production chain, as well as those engaged on the science.

Printed in the UK by The Stationery Office Limited
on behalf of the Controller of Her Majesty's Stationery Office
ID5958586   01/09   417733

Printed on Paper containing 75% recycled fibre content minimum.